Discovering
Rutland Epitaphs

ISBN: 0 9524544 6 7

The front cover design is based on the south doorway of
Egleton church. The photograph on the back cover is of
Hambleton church.

Printed by: Proprint, 13 The Metro Centre, Welbeck Way,
Peterborough PE2 7UH

Discovering
Rutland Epitaphs

Collected & Arranged
By
Bryan Waites

MULTUM
IN PARVO
PRESS
Oakham, Rutland

2006

Publications of Multum in Parvo Press

Celebration of Rutland (out of print)

Rutland Trails

Monasteries and Landscape in North East England

Normanton Tower Rutland Water

All Saints' Oakham: a guide and history

Paul's Poems: Reflections of a Teenager

Rutland Epitaphs

Also available through Multum in Parvo Press:-

Oakham Heritage Trail

Remember Rutland

Rutland Heritage

Rutland Alphabet

All enquiries: 01572 722893
Published by Multum in Parvo Press,
6 Chater Road, Oakham, Rutland LE15 6RY, England

CONTENTS

This book is dedicated to the late Peter Weight of Oakham School – husband, father, scholar, teacher, actor, singer, musician and much more

FOREWORD

A book on epitaphs! How macabre you may say. But in no way is this a mawkish trail through the churches and churchyards of Rutland. The underlying assumption in these holy places is that everything, birth, life, death and beyond, are all in the merciful hands of God. The churches themselves are a sign of his presence with his people, a sign that there is a meaning and purpose to all that goes on. And these memorials often reflect that faith.

Here Bryan Waites has assembled for us a remarkable array of vignettes: little character studies, mini-biographies, poetic homilies of the people of our villages over the last five hundred years, all engraved in stone. Many epitaphs are in danger of erosion by weather....some are no longer legible. Bryan Waites has done us a great service in ensuring that these are not lost.

But he has also given us the opportunity to hear the voices of the past, voices which give us clues as to how our forebears coped with bereavement, what their values were, what they believed about life and death, their thoughts, their feelings, their sentiments. I very much hope that the present churchyard regulations do not stifle such creative tributes from to-day's bereaved relatives and friends.

To wander around a churchyard where our 'rude forefathers' lie, some who have no memorial, others with a grandeur out of all proportion to their importance, to see the wild life, to reflect on the stream of humanity which has enriched our lives... all this puts our own life into some sort of perspective.

The Churchyard at St Mary's Manton Rutland

I hope this book will encourage its readers to enjoy the churches and churchyards of Rutland. It is a mine of intriguing facts and detail, an invitation to find out more about the place where we live, and maybe a starting point for further serious research.

We can only be grateful to Bryan Waites for this exciting addition to his already considerable publications about Rutland.

Revd. Charles Mayhew Former Vicar of Oakham with Hambleton, Egleton, Braunston and Brooke Canon Emeritus of Peterborough Cathedral

William Hibbin's tombstone St Mary's Ketton showing his masons tools

INTRODUCTION

I suppose I have a vested interest in churchyards, gravestones and epitaphs being an old man and in sight of Paradise. Can you believe that there is a delight in hunting for epitaphs? You might meet an old friend recently departed or someone you knew distantly or even a famous person you never met.

There are surprises such as the man with five wives, the last one of whom survived him; someone killed in a bayonet charge at Gallipoli; a clergyman who won the VC in the Afghan War; the Wise Woman of Wing or a memory of the Airborne Division at Arnhem or perhaps just someone who 'loved his village'.

Epitaphs may be carved on a variety of stones many of which weather so much that they can't be read. Slate (in this area Swithland Slate from Charnwood Forest) is best because the inscription is more or less permanent. However, as you travel further east across the county there are fewer slate gravestones. Occasionally there may be a cast iron 'tombstone' as at Langham and Ashwell. Italian white marble stones came in only relatively recently and to-day polished granite tombstones with sandblast and incised lettering in gold are becoming the norm. Diocesan regulations are still very strict and so the variety of stones is fairly limited.

There are epitaphs inside churches as well as outside but on the whole I have ignored factual memorials and dedications unless they include an epitaph. Also stained glass windows often contain dedications which are not epitaphs. There may be grave slabs on the floor of churches which may have an epitaph but even here the passage of many feet over the centuries erodes the lettering.

Rutland is small enough to allow full coverage of all its parish churches. I have visited all 49 but did not visit chapels or council cemeteries. Some churchyards had little to offer but others had an abundance of epitaphs. I have arranged my selection alphabetically via village churches for ease in visiting. Most churches are kept open during the day but if closed there is usually a notice to say who holds the key. Luckily, the churchyard is always available.

The earliest tombstones date from the 1600s and they are small and stocky with little inscribed on them. Ashwell has a few of these. Inscriptions improve with the tombstones of the 18th and 19th centuries which offer more scope – people seemed to want to write more. Often, however, this may be a biblical text, but I have not collected these. Occasionally recent tombstones have good epitaphs. Just as flowers are strewn around an accident site so now people, though not religious, are becoming more demonstrative and want to express what they feel on an inscription.

Of course, tombstones are an historical record giving as they do names, family details, relationships, ages, sometimes occupations and if the person died suddenly or in odd circumstances. The ceremonial art of the gravestone is also instructive. In Ketton churchyard the Hibbins family of stonemasons show the tools of their trade on their gravestones. The orientation of graves, their distribution, the shape of the churchyard and other factors are all relevant but I am sticking simply to recording my own selection of epitaphs and not venturing into this wider field of enquiry.

I have dedicated this book to the late Peter Weight of Oakham School – husband, father, teacher, actor, singer, musician and much more. In a conversation long ago he told me he was collecting epitaphs for use in his teaching of English. I encouraged him to think of putting them into a book when he was ready, but he died at a youngish age soon after. I was never able to find his collection of epitaphs, which I regret, so years later I decided to undertake the task myself.

I hope this book will encourage you to go searching for epitaphs in Rutland and beyond. I expect I have missed many which are waiting for you to find. There is a great joy in just looking. It will get you into the fresh air and you will discover much about the human condition –

'The still, sad music of humanity,
Nor harsh nor grating, though of ample power
To chasten and subdue'

You will need a kneeler of some sort, it is hard crouching down for a long time copying an inscription. A stiff brush is needed to clean grass off the tombstone. A notebook, pen, stout shoes – there are many ankle-twisting subsidence holes and rough ground. Some churchyards are closed, like All Saints' Oakham (closed in 1860) but you may still find tombstones laid horizontally. In too many churchyards the tombstones have been relegated to line up around the walls. This has happened at Lyndon. The famous artist, John Piper, deplores this which he describes as:

'set in guilty-looking rows, like children who have misbehaved, against the walls of church or churchyard......which militates against enjoyable epitaph-hunting, and against the beauty of churchyards'.

Copy the epitaphs **exactly** as you see them. Do not ignore **recent tombstones**. Inside churches can be very gloomy so a torch is useful. Also, binoculars are handy for high level epitaphs on wall tablets and of course a camera will be needed especially as you can photograph a very long epitaph to save you recording time. Expect to have difficulty finding and reading inscriptions. Frequently, inscriptions have been weathered away and you will have to look long and hard at the rest. Mostly, I have copied the punctuation exactly although it is often absent or eccentric. There are grammatical errors which I have usually left alone.

I have concentrated on churches and churchyards but you can look for epitaphs in non-conformist chapels, school chapels, Quaker burial grounds, etc. even in very odd places such as Morcorey Wood, near the A1, where a horse is commemorated. Of course, animal epitaphs introduce a whole new spectrum!!

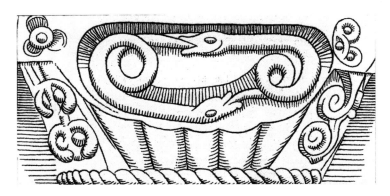

Tower arch capital at Morcott church

Rutland Epitaphs

'Let us now praise famous men, and our fathers that begat us.....There be of them, that have left a name behind them. And some there be, which have no memorial' *Ecclesiasticus*

Ashwell St Mary

I was so sore with Pain oppress'd
It wore my strength away
And made me long for heavenly rest
That never will decay
Susanna Harris d. Oct 8th 1835 Aged 71

In deep distress and troubled thoughts
To thee my GOD I raised my cries
If thou severely mark our Faults
No flesh can stand before thine Eyes
Jn. Dunmore Gent. d. 12th May 1788 Aged 53

Short was his race long is his rest
God takes them soon whom he loves best
James son of Tho.Sketh d. May 22nd 1717

How blest the Man forever blest
Whose guilt is pardon'd by his GOD
Whose Sins with Sorrow are confes'd
And cover'd with his Saviour's Blood
Robt Dunmore Gent. d. 9th January 1789

I AM I, AND
YOU ARE YOU
WHAT EVER WE WERE
TO EACH OTHER
THAT WE STILL ARE
JOHN W.
THWAITES
1917-1994

WEEP NOT DEAR FRIENDS BUT BE CONTENT
FOR UNTO YOU I WAS BUT LENT
JESUS HAS BOUGHT ME WITH HIS BLOOD
AND TOOK ME WHEN HE THOUGHT IT GOOD
GEORGE MASON d. MAY 31st 1878 Aged 70

JESUS, THY PERFECT RIGHTEOUSNESS
MY BEAUTY IS MY GLORIOUS DRESS.
MIDST FLAMING WORLDS IN THIS ARRAY'D
WITH JOY SHALL LIFT UP MY HEAD
WHEN FROM THE DUST OF DEATH I RISE
TO TAKE MY MANSION IN THE SKIES.
E'EN THEN SHALL THIS BE ALL MY PLEA
JESUS HATH DIED AND LIVES FOR ME
*JOHN TIDD WHO DIED AT STAMFORD
OCTOBER 20th 1890 Aged 82*

Reserved
By
G.G.WHEELER

Ayston St Mary

She's gone alas whose death we all lament.
Tho' death's a blessing to a life well spent.
Let not this vain world your thoughts employ.
But think this day: the last you may enjoy
Mary Goodwin d. June 11th 1833 Aged 28 years

Grieve not dear friends but be Content
Because to you I was but Lent.
My days was short like winter sun
To Earth I came to Heaven I Run
Thomas Mason d. February 1st 1839 Aged 24 years

FOR WE MUST NEEDS DIE AND ARE
AS WATER SPILT ON THE GROUND
WHICH CANNOT BE GATHERED
UP AGAIN NEITHER DOTH GOD
RESPECT ANY PERSON
Jane Hull born March 3rd 1791 d. June 3rd 1866

FATHER IN THY TENDER KEEPING
LEAVE WE NOW OUR LOVED ONE SLEEPING
Mary Ann Tookey d. Sept 9th 1903 Aged 38 years

*The Fludyer and Finch families are buried in this
churchyard*

Barrowden St Peter

A sudden loss, a shock severe,
To part with him, we loved so dear.
It was God's will, it shall be so,
At His command, we all must go
John Frederick Preston Story
d.April 13th 1927 Aged 28 Years

With my two Babes here I repose
Our bed composed of Clay
With Dust our Bodies are inclos'd
Until the final Day
Since our good friend serenely sleeps
Within the silent grave
Elizabeth, wife of Thomas Bates,
d.February 1st 1830 Aged 32 Years
also William and Thomas their sons
who died infants inter'd with their mother

Belton-in-Rutland St Peter

Our life hangs by a slender thread,
Which soon is cut and we are dead;
Then reader, boast not of thy might;
We're here at noon and gone at night
Mary Goodliffe d. April 29th 1851
Aged 71 Years

Live to die and die to live
Mr Francis Kemp d. 2nd March 1826
Aged 79 Years

With serious thoughts, Spectator view thy fate,
Thus mortals pass to an immortal state;
Thro' death's dark vale we hope she's found the way
To the bright regions of eternal day
Frances Darnell d. July 26th 1839
In the 65th year of her age

BOLD INFIDELITY TURN PALE AND
BENEATH THIS STONE THREE HAPLESS INFANTS LIE
SAY, ARE THEY LOST OR SAVED:
IF DEATH'S BY SIN, THEY SINN;D FOR THEY LIE HERE
IF HEAVEN;S BY WORKS IN HEAVEN THEY CANT
APPEAR
AH REASON; HOW DEPRAVE;D
REVERE THE SACRED PAGE THE KNOT;S UNTYD
THEY DIED FOR ADAM SINN;D, THEY LIVE
FOR JESUS DIED
Thomas Henry d. March 27th 1853, 5 months
Henry Thomas d. September 15th 1854. 6 months
Alfred Jelley d. September 8th 1855, 7 months

Think of her fate revere the heavenly hand
That in its wisdom snatch'd her from below;
Long at her couch stern Death took not his stand
But fiercely menac'd and gave swift the blow
Say are ye sure his mercy shall extend
To you so long a space?
Alas! Ye Sigh!
Make then, while yet ye may your GOD your friend
And learn, with equal ease to sleep or die!
*Mrs Hannah Neal who in the pangs of childbirth resigned
her soul
into the hands of her Creator March 15th 1807 Aged 41
Years*

NEAR THIS PLACE INTERRED THERE LIES,
ONE WHOM THE QUAKERS DID DESPISE.
HIS POVERTY EARNED HIM DISGRACE,
THEY DENIED HIM A BURIAL PLACE:
THOUGH BY HIS FRIEND, IT HATH BEEN SAID,
TOWARDS A BURYING PLACE LARGE SUMS WERE
PAID,
POOR ROBERT MIGHT NOT THERE BE LAID.
OH FRIENDS, HOW COULD YOU BE SO HARD,
TO LET HIM LIE IN THIS CHURCHYARD;
A PLACE YOU ALL DISLIKE, WE KNOW
HOW COULD YOU DISPLACE A BROTHER SO,
IN MEMORY HERE THIS STONE DOTH STAND,
OF ROBERT, THE SON OF JOHN AND SARAH
SWANN.
IN ONE THOUSAND SEVEN HUNDRED AND FORTY
NINE
HE DID HIS SOUL TO GOD RESIGN
Robert Swann d. 1749. The gravestone is almost illegible

Bisbrooke St John the Baptist

Peacefully sleeping resting at last
Life's weary trials and troubles past
In silence he suffered in patience he bore
Til GOD called him home to suffer no more
Edward Bird d. May 26th *1920 Aged 56*

A ling'ring illness did me seize,
That wore my strength away;
And made me long for endless rest,
That never will decay.
Ann Tomblin d. April 7th *1834 Aged 31 Years*

From this hard Journey where on earth
Her soul has taken flight
And gone a Journey much more worth
To meet the Lord of light.
Jemima Tomlin d. March 6th *1819 Aged 63 Years*

Here lies the body of Nathaniel Clark,
Who never did no harm in light or dark;
But in his Blessed horses taken great delight,
And often travelled with them by day and night
*A four wheeled wagon led by four horses is carved on the
top of the
monument. Nathaniel, a local farmer, was killed in 1813
when thrown out of a
cart. The inscription is barely legible.*

Braunston-in-Rutland All Saints

Hope looks beyond the bounds of time
When what we now deplore
Shall rise in full immortal prime
And bloom to fade no more
William Hill d. 1805 Aged 73

Killed in a bayonet charge near Krithia in the
Gallipoli Peninsula on August 6th 1915
George Barrett Lieut. 12th Royal Warwickshire Regiment
born in
Braunston Vicarage

Evan Robert Hanbury Major Leics Yeomanry
attached to the Machine Gun Corps who was killed
in action near St Quentin 23rd March 1918 Aged 30.
This tablet is placed here by his mother.
More life and fuller

19669 MEMBER
GLADYS WALTER
Women's Royal Air Force
11TH November 1918 Aged 20
*This is a mystery. Why did she die on Armistice Day? Why
so young? The RAF was only formed in April 1918. Was
there a women's branch already?*

Brooke St Peter

Charles
Son of Andrew Noel brave and high
His dust inhabits here his soul the sky.
Nature and Worth, Valour and Wisdom too
In this one boy strove all their gifts to show
Worth made him duteous: Nature, a comely youth
Mars to be brave: bright Wisdom, loving truth
Yet even he in youth's fair springtime
pined
As buds will perish in a bitter wind
He died in 1619 at the age of 28 years

Burley-on-the-Hill Holy Cross

In all the duties of domestic and
Social life, as a daughter, as a wife, as a parent, as the
mistress of
a family, as the benefactress of the poor, the uprightness of
her
mind, the tenderness of her heart, the equanimity of her
temper,
and the gentleness of her disposition, were remarkable as
her
piety, her resignation and her trust in God were entire and
uniform....
She deserved and obtained the esteem
And confidence of her Sovereign, the almost filial affection
of her
Royal Pupils and the rare tribute of general approbation.

Honoured and beloved beyond the common lot of mortals,
she
Closed a life of Christian excellence, an object of devoted
attachment
And tender regret. In testimony of honour, love and
Veneration for the tenderest and best of mothers this
monument
Was erected by her grateful and affectionate son
Rt. Hon. Lady Charlotte Finch d. St James Palace 11th July
1813 aged 88
Years and 5 months. Sometime Governess of the Royal
Children of
George III

He was a true Christian
An Ornament to his Profession, a sincere Friend
And in every Character of Life
A worthy Honest Man
Revd William Hardy d. 23rd October 1752 in the 34th Year of
his Age

Trust not in friends and kindred
Neither put off the care of thy soul till
Thereafter for men will sooner forget thee
Than thou art aware of
Robert Wright d. April 22nd 1813 Aged 41 years

Farewell dear Wife and Children dear also
It was God's will that I should from you go
We part in grief yet hope to meet again
In Heav'n with joy for ever to remain
John Mays d. October 7th 1814 Aged 45 years

A loving babe lies sleeping here,
Was much belov'd by parents dear
Sweet babe he great affliction bore
But now is blest for evermore.
George Knight d. December 28th 1835 Aged 4 years

*There are many Finch graves on the north side of the
churchyard but no epitaphs*

Caldecott St John

Daily our mortal flesh decays.
But Christ our life shall come.
His unresisted power shall raise.
Our Bodys from the Tomb
William Morris d. March 28th 1825 Aged 84 years

Heav'n gives us friends to bless the present scene:
Receives them, to prepare us for the next.
All, all is right, by GOD ordained or done:
Rebecca Muggleton d. June 20th 1828 Aged 17 years

Blessed be the hand Divine
That Gently laid my head beneath
This doleful shade
*Rebecca Laxton wife of Thomas Laxton d. August 8th 1828
Aged 44 years*

Laurels may flourish round the conq'rors tomb
But happiest they who win the world to come
Eternal triumphs crown their toils divine
And all those triumphs now we trust are thine
Ann Morris d. February 13th 1832 Aged 22 years

Children farewell you also must
Turn like your parents dust to dust.
Yet from the dust our God shall raise
His ransom'd to shew forth his praise
Robert Morris d. September 25th 1851 Aged 72 years

There are some fine table tombs of the Stokes family in the churchyard

Clipsham St Mary

When Death was sent from Heaven above,
To part Our Unity and Love,
No Friend, nor yet Physicions Art,
Could then prevent his fatall Dart,
I was with him and He must be,
In a short Time in Dust with Me
Esther Russell d. Mar 9th 1738/9 Aged 34 years. Why the split year?

I was so long with pain oppress'd,
That wore my strength away,
It made me wish for endless rest,
That never will decay
Melicent Wright d. April 5th 1831 Aged 54 years

Cottesmore St Nicholas

Farewell vain world I've had enough of thee
I value not what thou can'st say of me
What fault thou'st see in me take care to show
Go look at home there's something to be done
William Laxton d. June 24th 1708 Aged 68

WHEN YOU LAY ME TO
SLUMBER
NO SPOT COULD CHOOSE
BUT WOULD SING TO THE RHYTHM
OF GALLOPING SHOES
AND UNDER THE DAISIES NO
GRAVE BE SO DEEP
BUT THE HOOFS OF THE
HORSES WILL SOUND IN MY SLEEP
*'Uncle' Edward Chapman Clayton 1837-1936 a famous
hunting man*

Edith Weston St Mary the Virgin

He was a Man of a most amiable
Disposition, a good Christian of sound
Learning and strict Integrity
*Revd Richard Lucas DD Prebend of Canterbury & Rector d.
Jan 17th 1789 Aged 64*

After a long and Painful Illness
Which she bore with most exemplary
Patience and entire resignation to the
Divine Will departed this Life
3rd November 1790 Aged 69
Martha Relict of the Revd Dr Lucas

Lady MARGARET HEATHCOTE,
Second Daughter of
PHILIP Earl of HARDWICKE,
Lord High Chancellor of Great Britain
And wife of
SIR GILBERT HEATHCOTE Baronet
A Lady, who
by the Elegance of her Mind,
and all the Virtues, which adorn
the different characters she sustained
of Daughter, Wife, Friend and Mistress,
merited and secured
the Regard and Esteem of all who approached her
She was born March the 21st 1733,
Was marry'd June the 22nd 1749,
and dy'd after a long state of ill health,
in childbed, August the 19th 1769

To the
Memory of Sir GILBERT HEATHCOTE Knt and Bart
A Person of Great Natural Endowments, improved by long
Experience,
Ready to Apprehend, Slow to Determine, Resolute to Act;
A Zealous Friend to the Rights and Libertys of Mankind;
In Offices of Power and Trust, True to his own and
Countrys Honour

A Great Instrument in Founding, and well Governing, the
Bank of England;
In the Year 1711 was Lord Mayor of London,
Which City he Governed with Courage, and Temper.
After Leaving Represented it in four successive Parliaments,
With Dignity, and Integrity, from the Year 1701.
A Kind Landlord, a Steady Friend, an Affectionate Relation;
In his Character unblemished;
In his Extensive Trade without a Lawsuit
Died 1733

Sir GILBERT HEATHCOTE BARONET
He was a Man of the strictest integrity of heart
Most unaffected humility of mind
And a temper and manner truly humane and gentle
His greatest happiness consisted in the domestic scene
And in all his relative duties he was kind and affectionate
Died 2nd December 1785. Aged 64. *The above memorials were
removed from Normanton church during the construction of Rutland
Water and placed in St Mary's*

Egleton St Edmund

So much at least is due
from Filial piety
To the memory of tender
and affectionate parents
*Mary Dain wife of John Dain d. 16th Sept 1768 aged 54
years*

Forbear, my friends to weep
Since death hath lost its sting
Those Christians that in Jesus sleep,
Our God will with him bring
Thomas Thomson d. 21 March 1779 Aged 70

See then that ye walk circumspectly,
not as fools but as wise
Redeeming the time because
the days are evil
Tho Croft of Gunthorpe d. 27 October 1756 Aged 73

Scholar,musician
actress & artist
light as dreams
tough as oak
precious as gold
Aged 20 (2002)

Empingham St Peter

Was kind and gentle, endowed with ev'ry Care
Which do Adorn and bless, a single state;
O greet her Ashes with a friendly Tear
With us lament a loss which is so great
Elizabeth Collington d. November 4th 1786 Aged XLVI

LIFE'S RACE WELL RUN
LIFE'S WORK WELL DONE
LIFE'S CROWN WELL WON
NOW COMES REST
EDWARD SNEATH d. SEPT 1st 1880 AGED 86 YEARS

Essendine St Mary

Within this Grave enclosed here one lies
Who in her Lifetime sought the only Prize
The one thing needful that desired She
To live with Christ to all Eternity
Mary Relict of Jarvis Osborn d. June 12th 1781 Aged 64
years

Exton St Peter & St Paul

NOW WHEN THE FATES HAVE BID US TO
HAVE DONE WITH LIFE AND THE STARS
DEMAND OUR SPIRITS, THE AFFECTION
OF OUR HEIR HAS GATHERED OUR
ASHES AND BIDDEN THEM REST
UNDER THIS MAUSOLEUM
Sir James (d.1591) and Lady Harington

….A Lady endowed with a natural
disposition to Vertue, a true understanding of honour, most
noble
behaviour, perpetual cheerfulness, most eligant
Conversation, and
a more than ordinary conjugal affection. She was married iv.
years and ix. months, and left only one child named Robert
Bruce.

Weakened by that birth she died in Childbirth, the xx. day of March, in the xxii. year of her age, Anno Domini MDC XXVII.
Erected and inscribed to the memory of his most beloved deserving Wife, by Tho. Lord Bruce

.........his Hospitality and Liberality to all that desir'd or deserved it (notwithstanding inestimable Losses in His Estate, frequent
Imprisonment of his Person, Spoil and Havock of several of his
Houses, besides the Burning of that noble Pile of CAMPDEN) have
Justly rendred him the Admiration of his Contempories, and the Imitation of Posterity. He left this Life for the Exchange and Fruition of a better, the 29th day of October, in the LXXI
of his Age A.D. MDCLXXXIII
BAPTIST NOEL LORD VISCOUNT CAMPDEN, BARON OF RIDLINGTON AND ILMINGTON

To NAMES like These, it is unnecessary to add
any Praise, as they will be long remembered Here
with LOVE, with VENERATION, and with GRATITUDE
*Baptist, 4th EARL of GAINSBOROUGH d .MARCH 21st
1751 Aged 43 Years. Elizabeth, his WIFE d. Dec 15th 1771
Aged 64 & THOMAS NOEL ESQ OF WALCOT d. June 18th
1788 Aged 83 Years*

A FRIEND TO PEACE, A FOE TO STRIFE,
IS HERE TO EARTH CONSIGN'D;
MISFORTUNES CHAS'D HIM THROUGH THIS LIFE,
A BETTER LIFE TO FIND

HE RESTS IN PEACE, AND SWEETEST HOPE,
THAT HE SHALL BE FORGIVEN;
AND TRUST'S HIS SAVIOUR'S MERIT DEAR
WILL PLEAD HIS CAUSE IN HEAVEN

AND WHEN THE ANGELS TRUMP SHALL SOUND,
HE HOPES WITH JOY TO RISE;
THEN ALL SHALL KNOW MISFORTUNES HERE,
ARE BLESSINGS IN DISGUISE
Stephen Messing d. 26th Jan 1831 Aged 66 years

Joyful, courageous and loving of heart
fervent in spirit serving the LORD
he brought men to CHRIST
GOD is love and he that dwelleth in love
dwelleth in GOD and GOD in him
MONTAGUE WRIOTHESLEY NOEL
Commander RN d. April 6th 1941
While on convoy duty in the English Channel

WHEN PICTURES LOOK ALIVE
WITH MOVEMENT FREE
WHEN SHIPS LIKE FISHES
SWIM BENEATH THE SEA,
WHEN MEN OUT STRIPPING BIRDS
CAN SCAN THE SKY,
THEN HALF THE WORLD DEEP DRENCHED
IN BLOOD SHALL BE
MAJOR TERENCE ANDREW ALFRED WATT, LIFE
GUARDS Killed while flying on active service July 17th
1942

AS LADY WARRENDER SHE LIVED AT
EXTON FROM 1928 TO 1935
AND EARNED THE AFFECTION
AND RESPECT OF THE PARISH
HER REMAINS NOW REST IN THE
CHURCHYARD AND HER HAPPIEST DAYS
WERE SPENT IN THIS COUNTRYSIDE
RIP
DOROTHY ETTA d. 1st July 1975 In Her 77th YEAR (The
daughter of Col RH
Rawson)

Glaston St Andrew

Gone from us but not forgotten
Never shall thy memory fade
Sweetest thoughts shall ever linger
Round the spot where thou art laid
Susannah Rate d. May 26th 1900 Aged 63

WHEN THE DAY OF TOIL IS DONE
WHEN THE RACE OF LIFE IS RUN
FATHER GRANT THY WEARIED ONES
REST FOR EVERMORE
Samuel Stevens d. Nov 28th 1926 Aged 71 years

Teach us delight in simple things
And mirth that hath no bitter springs
Ronald & Josephine Townsend 1912-94; 1918-95

*There are two memorials in the church to Lieut. The Hon.
C.M.Evans-Freke, 16th Queen's Lancers who died in the
Transvaal in 1900 and Lieut. Col.The Hon.Percy Cecil
Evans-Freke who fell in action near Ypres in 1915.*

Great Casterton St Peter & St Paul

GENEROUS, CHARITABLE AND GOOD
HE BUILT AND ENDOWED THE CHURCH
AT PICKWORTH, AND DID ALL IN HIS
POWER FOR THE BENEFIT OF HIS
PARISHIONERS
WHO BUILDS A CHURCH TO GOD AND NOT TO
FAME
WILL NEVER MAR THE MARBLE WITH HIS NAME
The Revd Richard Lucas M.A. d. May 9th 1827

BOAST NOT THYSELF OF TOMORROW
FOR THOU KNOWEST NOT WHAT TODAY
MAY BRING FORTH
Samuel Peet d. 18th May 1889 Aged 75 years

HER LIFE WAS ENDED BY AN ACCIDENT AND
HER SPIRIT RETURNED TO GOD JULY 30TH 1896
Violet Cecilia Hardy Sellman Aged 6 years

O DEATH NO MORE NO MORE DELAY
MY SPIRIT LONGS TO FLEE AWAY
AND BE AT REST;
THE WILL OF HEAVEN MY WILL SHALL BE
I BOW TO THE DIVINE DECREE,
TO GOD'S BEHEST

*Martha Cole Stretton d. February 20th 1916 Aged 82 years
John Clare, the Peasant Poet, was married in this church to
his 'Sweet Patty of the Vale', 20th March 1820, but he is
buried at Helpston.*

Little Casterton All Saints

IN LIFE HE FILLED THE UNFORGIVING MINUTE
WITH SIXTY SECONDS WORTH OF DISTANCE RUN
IN DEATH HIS LEGACY OF FAITH, HOPE AND LOVE
WILL LIVE WITH US FOREVER
REST NOW IN PEACE WITH GOD MY LOVE
(2004)

FARMER & COUNTRYMAN
(2005)

Greetham St Mary

My flesh shall slumber in the ground
Whilst the last joyful trumpet sound
And then awake with great surprise
And in my Saviour's image rise
Thomas Sharman d. December 21st 1786 Aged LXVII

Through life thy virtues were our joy and pride,
Our best example and our safest guide.
In death we mourn thee; yet, resigned to Heaven.
(That takes, in mercy, what was lent – not given)
Our tears, by faith and hope are wiped away,
Till we rejoin thee in eternal day.
John Bellaers late of Hodby Lodge d. 13th Feb 1843 Aged 70 years

GONE FROM US, BUT NOT FORGOTTEN
NEVER SHALL THEIR MEMORY FADE,
SWEETEST THOUGHTS WILL EVER LINGER
ROUND THE SPOT WHERE THEY ARE LAID
Samuel Spencer d. Feb 20th 1909 Aged 49 and Harriet d. Jan 7th 1928 Aged 67

Sunshine passes shadows
fall but loving memories
outlast them all
Bernard Royce Marshall d. Nov 14th 1983 Aged 64 years

Hambleton St Andrew

Under a spreading chestnut tree
The village smithy stands
(Longfellow)
Richard York Ireland
A dear husband and loving father
Died 9th July 2001
Aged 83 years

In Memory
Of Matthew Woodcock
Who died April 21st 1877
Aged 68 Years
AMELIA, WIFE OF THE ABOVE
WHO DIED MAY 24TH 1863
Amelia was known as 'The Wise Woman of Wing'

According to the church guide, Sir Malcolm Sargent's daughter is buried in the churchyard. He married the niece of Mrs Astley Cooper who owned Hambleton Hall.
The tomb with a tall lantern cross near the gate is that of Walter Gore Marshall (brewery magnate) who built Hambleton Hall in 1881 and made many improvements to both church and village in the 1890s. His sister was Mrs Astley Cooper who occupied the Hall after her brother's death.

Ketton St Mary

This world is nothing Heaven is all,
Death did not kill mee by my fall,
Goe tell my Frends that for mee weep
I am not dead but here do sleep.
Richard Spencer d. November 20th MDCCXXIII
Aged 51 years

Sacred to the Memory of
ANTHONY HOTCHKIN
Grocer and Citizen of London
Who in the Midst of Life and a very
Gainful Trade, satisfied with
Moderate Acquisitions,
Retired Here from the hurry of Business
To the quiet Enjoyment of Himself,
His Friends, and Fortune.
Affording a rare Instance of Contentment
But alas; a very common one
Of Human Disappointment.
He was seized with a lingering Illness
That put a period to his Life Feb 19, 1763
In the 48th Year of his Age
This is a floor slab

UNIVERSALLY BELOVED HONOURED AND
LAMENTED
STEPHEN EATON
DIED AT KETTON HALL
25TH SEPT 1834 AGED 54 YEARS
There is a longer epitaph with this

......Friend and Guide to all in Sorrow or difficulty needed
Aid or Sympathy Ever Generous and Forgiving she was
gifted with great Intellect
Untiring Energy; but her Resignation and Patience, under
long continued Suffering
Shed a brighter Lustre over the many Virtues of her acts in
Life which had been one long Devotion to the good of
Others................
Her epitaph is writ in the Hearts of the Poor:
And All who knew her mourn a Friend.....................
Charlotte Ann Eaton of Ketton Hall d. in London April 28th
1859 Aged 70 years

Langham St Peter & St Paul

His influence diffused itself imperceptibly around him
like some rare spirit moving on the face of the waters.....
the modesty, simplicity and beauty of his daily life, his
chivalrous consideration for the feelings of others
and his wholly unselfish interests.........
Sir Henry Clarke Jervoise Bt d. 2nd March 1908. This is part
of a framed eulogy hanging on the wall inside the church

MAJOR GENERAL LORD RANKSBOROUGH CB, CVO
LATE COMMANDER ROYAL HORSE GUARDS
LORD LIEUTENANT OF RUTLAND
BORN 1859 DIED 1921
SERVED IN EGYPTIAN CAMPAIGNS AND
COMMANDED
THE 3RD CAVALRY BRIGADE IN THE BOER WAR
1900
EQUERRY TO QUEEN VICTORIA AND QUEEN
ALEXANDRA
HE GAVE FAITHFUL SERVICE TO GOD, KING AND
COUNTRY
AND WAS GREATLY BELOVED BY ALL
ERECTED BY HIS WIDOW

IN
PROUD REMEMBRANCE OF
THE
OFFICERS AND MEN
OF THE
FIRST AIRBORNE
DIVISION
WHO JOINED THE WORSHIP
WITH THE PARISHIONERS
IN THIS CHURCH
FROM HERE THEY WENT TO
ARNHEM
WHERE BETWEEN THE 17TH
AND 25TH SEPTEMBER
1944 MANY OF THEM
LAID DOWN THEIR LIVES
IN GOD
WAS THEIR STRENGTH

He loved his village
ARTHUR (Archie) SHELTON born 19 June 1906
d. 7th January 1992

Wanted on voyage
CHARLES LITTLE d. 4 January 2000 Aged 77 years

Simon de Langham (1310-1376), Abbot of Westminster Abbey,
Treasurer of England, Lord Chancellor, Archbishop of Canterbury and
Cardinal has strong links with this place but his tomb is in the Abbey.
Both Sir Kenneth and Lady Ruddle are buried in the churchyard

North Luffenham St John the Baptist

Robert Johnson
Bachelor Of Divinitie,
A Painful Preacher,
Parson of North Luffenham
Had a Godlie Charge Of Religion,
And A Charitable Minde To The Poore.
He erected a faire free grammar schoole in Okeham,
He erected a faire free grammar schoole in Uppingham
He appointed to each of his schooles a schoolmaster and an
usher,
He erected the Hospitalle of Christe in Okeham,
He erected the Hospitalle of Christe in Uppingham.

He was also Beneficiall ToTheTown Of North
Luffenham, And Also To The Towne Of Stamford
Where he Was Borne Of Worshipfull
Parents..............
It Is The Grace Of God To Give A Man A Wise
Harte To Lay Up His Treasure in Heaven........
Let Your Light So Shine
Archdeacon Robert Johnson (1541 – 1625)

Samuel Winter Dr of Divinity Eminent for piety
& learning late Provost of Trinity
Colledge neare Dubline
d. 24th Dec 1666 Aged 63 years

Think now as softly sad you tread
Above the venerable Dead
Time was like full Life posest
And time will be when you shall rest
Anthony Jarratt d. Feb 11th 1754 in the 59th year of his age

Near this Place
Lye the Remains of JOHN DIGBY ESQ.
Lineally Descended from an Antient family
Whose Residence has been at this Town
Near Four Hundred Years.
He Married DEBORAH the Daughter
Of John FARDELL, Citizen
To Whom he was a tender
And Affectionate Husband,
And to his Memory She Erected ye Monument.
His Generous and Benevolent Temper
Rendered Him Beloved & His Death Lamented.
He died May the 19th 1758
In the 31st Year of his Age

IN MEMORY
OF OUR BELOVED SON
WHO GAVE HIS LIFE THAT
FREEDOM MIGHT LIVE
R.140521 Flt Sergeant
R H LEWIS
AIR GUNNER
Royal Canadian Airforce
27th Feb 1943 Age 23

HE WAS A SOLDIER AND A TEACHER TOO
AND FOR HIS MUSIC HE COMBINED THE TWO
HE TAUGHT GIRLS AND BOYS TO MAKE A JOYOUS
NOISE
George Christopher Young d. March 29th 1979

Vincent Wing (1619 – 1668), noted mathematician and astronomer, was buried in this churchyard. There are many graves of members of the Armed Forces, particularly RAF, RNZAF, RCAF and RAustAF serving at North Luffenham Air Base

South Luffenham St Mary

IN MEMORY OF
ROSE BOSWELL
DAUGHTER OF EDWARD AND SARAH BOSWELL
WHO DIED FEBRUARY 19TH 1794
AGE 17 YEARS
WHAT GRIEF CAN VENT THIS LOSS OR PRAISES
TELL,
HOW MEEK, HOW GOOD, HOW BEAUTIFUL SHE
FELL

Note in the parish register: 'the young woman was one of the people commonly called Gipsies, she was buried in the church and had a funeral sermon preached'. Described as a 'Gipsy Princess'

ALL EARTHLY COMFORTS VANISH THUS
SO LITTLE HOLD OF THEM HAVE WE
THAT WE FROM THEM OR THEY FROM US
MAY IN A MOMENT TAKEN BE
Edward Pridmore d. August ? 1838

Hope looks beyond the bounds of time
When what we now deplore
Shall rise in full immortal prime
And bloom to fade no more
Dorothy Royce d. Nov 15th 1850 in the 35th year of her age

REJOICE WE YET SHALL MEET AGAIN
WHERE NONE MAY SAY FAREWELL
AND IN ONE HOME OF DEATHLESS LOVE
TOGETHER WE SHALL DWELL
Sarah Pridmore d. Dec 25th 1867

Lyddington St Andrew

Within these graves two faithful friends confind
A loving Father and a Mother kind,
A tender Father and Mother's comforts here
Lamented by their children dear
Mourn not for us, but be content
Because to you we was but lent.
Thomas Dawson d. May 14th 1834 Aged 67 years and
Sarah, his wife, d. June 23rd 1841 Aged 73 years

HIS AMIABLE AND CHRISTIAN DEPORTMENT
WON THE ESTEEM AND ADMIRATION OF ALL WHO
KNEW HIM
AND HIS UNTIMELY DEATH
(WHICH WAS OCCASIONED BY AN ACCIDENT
ON BOARD THE SHIP IN WHICH HE WAS ABOUT TO
SAIL
FOR HIS NATIVE COUNTRY)
IS DEEPLY REGRETTED BY HIS SURVIVING
RELATIVES AND FRIENDS
Joseph Clarke d. December 27th 1843 Aged 46 years. His
remains were interred in Brooklyn Cemetery, New York,
North America

HE SPENT THE LATTER YEARS OF HIS LIFE
AT LYDDINGTON & DEVOTED HIMSELF
TO THE WELFARE OF THE VILLAGE
*Astley Vavasour Clarke JP, DL, MD, High Sheriff for
Rutland in 1942 d. 21ˢᵗ Feb 1945 Aged 75 years*

DIED AT LYDDINGTON 27ᵀᴴ JULY 1988
IN THE COUNTRY HE LOVED
Comte Henri de la Brière DFC
OFFICIER DE LA LEGION D'HONNEUR
CROIX DE GUERRE 4 PALMES
CROIX FRANCE LIBRE
BORN IN FRANCE

FOND FATHER
AND RENOWNED RESEARCHER
Reginald Walter Powell born 8ᵗʰ June 1903 died 1ˢᵗ March
1991

*There are fine memorials to Helyn Hardy, widow of Robert Hardy
(1486) and Edward Watson, Surveyor-General to the Bishops of
Lincoln, d. 1520. Both have Latin inscriptions.*

Lyndon St Martin

He conducted a long and most exemplary life
*Thomas Barker 'Father of English Meteorology' d.
December 1809 Aged 88 years*

41

He was forty years clerk of this place.
He sung his psalms, he's run his race.
He's closed his book, he's said Amen.
In Christ he hopes to rise again
John Barsby d. December 1st 1810 Aged 87 years

His writings shew
His unwearied study
and excessive knowledge
in various parts of literature.
His sufferings for conscience sake
prove his sincerity.
After a life spent
in piety towards God
and benevolent charity
towards man.
He rests in Hope
through the merits of Christ
of a joyful and blessed Resurrection
to eternal life
*Revd William Whiston MA d. August 22 1752 in the 85th
year of his age. He was a mathematician and theologian. He
died at Lyndon Hall. He was the grandfather of Thomas
Barker.*

Manton St Mary

Henry Smith Esq.
Lord of this Mannour. He
was Faithfull to his Friends
Just to his Neighbour and
Devout and Pious toward
GOD
d. Sept 20th 1716 Aged 71

HER extraordinary success
in Physick and her extensive
CHARITY to thousands of poor
people, make her loss universal
to the BRITISH NATION
Penelope, widow of Henry Smith Esq.
Died 'exceedingly lamented' Sept 13th 1727 Aged 57

ANOTHER SISTER HERE DOTH LIE
THAT LIVED IN PEACE AND UNITY
HER SOUL WE HOPE IS GONE TO REST
AND WITH THE LORD FOREVER BLEST
Mary Ann Naylor d. June 8th 1848 Aged 32

I SHALL PASS THROUGH THIS WORLD BUT ONCE. ANY
GOOD THING THEREFORE THAT I CAN DO, OR ANY KIND-
NESS THAT I CAN SHOW TO ANY HUMAN BEING, OR DUMB
ANIMAL, LET ME DO IT NOW. LET ME NOT DEFER IT, OR
NEGLECT IT, FOR I SHALL NOT PASS THIS WAY AGAIN
*Robert Heathcote Esq. of Leesthorpe & Manton born April
24th 1843 died July 15th 1917*

GIVE ME A LIGHT THAT I MAY TREAD
SAFELY INTO THE UNKNOWN
Dorothy Margaret Butterley Churchwarden. Died 1981

Market Overton St Peter & St Paul

This monumental stone when you have read
Consider well the slippery path you tread.
In Lifes short Span or, Times more precious round,
Nothing of Certainty there's to be found;
In Health, in Vigor, and in youthful Bloom.
One Moment brings you to your silent Tomb.
Some Chance unseen, some Stroke unthought by thee
May End thy Life and lay thee low as me
John Martin d. October 4th 1758 In the 70th year of his age

By an awful providence behold;
I was arrested on my Journey
In the career of life's uncertain maze,
Thus all my labours cease
And projects end
His death was occasioned by a fall
from a wagon
Thomas Cooke d. 12th day of September 1798 Aged 18 years

A guilty, weak and helpless
Woman
On thy kind arms I fall:
Be thou my Strength
and righteousness
My Jesus and my
all
Ann Brown d. May 22nd 1828

Resigned and Patient to the last she view'd
With calm submission her approaching fate,
And now far happier with her life renew'd
Free from the troubles of a mortal state
Ann Smith d. June 8th 1836 Aged 26 years

What faults you seen amiss
Then strive to shun
And look at home
Enough their's to be done
*John Willbourn d. August 3:1845 Also 1 son and 4
daughters who died in their infancy*

He loved all things true and beautiful
And willingly gave his life for GOD'S
cause, for his country and for us. His
body lies at La Gorgue, Estaires, France
'I thank my God upon every remembrance of you'
*2nd Lieut Vincent Sladen Wing, 65th Howitzer Battery RFA
killed in France 10th August 1917 Aged 19*

No greater love could ever be given
From our little Angel sent from Heaven
With love that melts the hardest heart
Our special boy
Set apart
*JACK MAXWELL OUR BRAVE LITTLE BOY
YOU CLOSED YOUR EYES 13TH JUNE 1992
AGED 4 YEARS*

Morcott St Mary

The Beautyfull: the Innocent die Young
See how the Just, the Virtuous and ye Strong
Here in Promiscuous dust together lie.
Reflect on this depart and learn to die
Thomas Yates d. January 15th MDCCLXV Aged 25 years

There's no protection that can save
Us mortals from the silent grave
But all mankind must yield there breath
Unto the False stroke of death
In love he liv'd in faith he died
His life was begg'd but was denied
CHARLES PRETTY d. April 23rd 1817 Aged 24 years

Oakham All Saints

Ann the daughter of Andrew Burton of Okeham Esq. Fellow
of Grayes Inn, departed this Life, June 19 A.D. 1642 Aged
15
Reader stand back; dull not this marble Shrine
With irreligious breath: the Stone's divine,
And does inclose a Wonder; Beauty, Wit,
Devotion, and virginity with it.
Which like a Lilly fainting in its prime
Wither'd and left the World; deceitful Time
Cropt it too soon; and Earth the self same Womb
From whence is sprung, is now become its Tomb.
Whose sweeter soul, a Flower of matchless price;
Transplanted is from hence to Paradice
Andreas & Anna Parentes PP *(quoted in Wright 1684)*

Full happy Man that dies in faith
His good works follow him Christ saith
Glad are his saints desolv'd to be,
To live with Christ his face to see
Francis Davie d. Jan 12 1717 Aged 67 years (floor slab)

Here lies beneath, from
A tender Mother, and a loving Wife
A quiet Neighbour, to the Poor a friend
Happy is she, who such a life doth lead
*Wife of John Bellaers of Barleythorpe d. 12th May
MDCCLXXXVI (floor slab)*

Vain in our pleasures vainer in our cares
Bound on the wheel of time we ride and fall
Yet present wrong Eternity repairs
The mighty empr'ss and the Judge of all
*Thomas Bullivant d. 29th April 1786 Aged 37 years (floor
slab)*

*Affliction sore long time I bore,
Physician skill was vain;
Till Christ; the chief sent me relief
And eas'd me of my pain.
John Bellaers d. August 18 MDCCCIX (floor slab)*

....................this stone is
here deposited by an only
Child, as the last but perishable
Memorial of one, who has
Seldom been surpassed,
as a tender parent,
an affectionate wife,
and a virtuous woman
*Mrs Dorothy Twentyman d. Feb 1809 Aged 60 years (floor
slab)*

From AD 1877 TO 1922 he devoted
His life to this Church as its organist
& choirmaster winning the love of all
MAY HE REST IN PEACE
Harry Nicholson by his many friends

Malcolm Sargent, when organist at St Mary's, Melton Mowbray, was a friend and frequent participant in the concerts organised by Harry (who lived in Flores House). For a time Malcolm lived at 19 Burley Road, Oakham.

Preston St Peter & St Paul

He was a Zealous Preacher
a Watchful Pastor Just to all
Loving to his neibor……….
Faithful to his friend……….
Devout and Pious toward God
& Strictly Carefull of his Soul
Aged 48 dyed March 7th 1690
John Hill MA Rector

In brief to speak her praise let this suffice,
She was a wife just, frugal, good and wise:
Of children careful, to her neighbours kind
All certain symptoms of a virtuous mind
Mary Whottoff d. 14th April 1780 Aged 71 years

In whom were listed
those amiable Qualifications
which rendered her
much respected in social life
and sincerely regretted
in Death
She left this mutable state
of Existence
3rd Feb 1795 Aged 63 years
Mary Mackley

NICHOLAS BATESON
Who grew happily to manhood in
this Parish and having qualified as a
Solicitor was killed at sea on March
31st 1955 during his National Service
with the Fleet Air Arm Aged 26
'He being made perfect in a short time
fulfilled a long time'

AND THIS OUR LIFE
EXEMPT FROM PUBLIC HAUNT
FINDS TONGUES IN TREES,
BOOKS IN THE RUNNING BROOKS,
SERMONS IN STONES,
AND GOOD IN EVERYTHING
DORIS HALFORD BALDWIN 1897-1983

Ridlington St Mary Magdalen & St Andrew

A SUDDEN CHANCE DEAR FRIENDS UPON ME FELL
I HAD NOT TIME TO BID YOU ALL FAREWELL
THINK NOTHING STRANGE, DEATH HAPPENS TO
US ALL
MY LOT TO-DAY, TO-MORROW YOURS MAY FALL
MATILDA LOUNT OCTOBER 17TH 1903 AGED 55 YEARS
WHO DIED (SUDDENLY)

Ryhall St John the Evangelist

He was a man of most amiable Disposition
A good Christian a Tender Husband
One of sound Learning and Strict Integrity

When on the Borders of the gloomy grave
Beyond all power of human Art to save
Calm and collected He resigned his breath.
Put off Mortality and smiled in Death
Thomas Harrison, Rector of Casterton Magna & Market Overton, late Vicar of this place d. 10th August 1782 Aged 87

The loss of time is much
The loss of much is more
The loss of Christ is such
The world cannot restore
THOMAS GANN NOV 5TH 1852 AGED 61 YEARS (very suddenly)

I LEAVE THE WORLD WITHOUT A TEAR
SAVE FOR THE FRIENDS I HELD SO DEAR;
TO HEAL THEIR SORROWS LORD DESCEND
AND TO THE FRIENDLESS PROVE A FRIEND
WILLIAM CULPIN d. JULY 17TH 1870 AGED 35 YEARS

WE CANNOT TELL WHO NEXT MAY FALL
BENEATH THY CHASTENING ROD
ONE MUST BE FIRST SO LET US ALL
PREPARE TO MEET OUR GOD
WILLIAM RINGHAM d. APRIL 5TH 1882 AGED 62 YEARS

Seaton All Hallows

ROBERT OVERTON
Born Easington Yorkshire
1609
died Seaton Rutland 1678
Scholar soldier and
family man, he held strong political and
religious beliefs. He rose to the rank of
Major General serving his God and country
for the cause of Parliament during the
English Civil War, He wrote 'if I can but
keep faith and a good conscience I shall
assuredly finish my course in joy'
*Presented by members of Col Robert Overton's Regiment of
Foote of the English Civil War Society in 1996*

How still and peaceful is the grave
When life's vain tumult's past
Th' appointed house by Heaven's Decree
Receives us all at Last
Frederick Knox d. April 16th 1866 Aged 54 years

A very fine tablet in the church to John Monckton and his family mentions links to the capture of Quebec (1759) and the American War of Independence. There is an enclosure in the churchyard for the same family.

Stoke Dry St Andrew

HERE LIETH THE BODY
OF DOROTHEY STEVENS
VIRGIN AGE XI WAITING
FOR A JOYFULL RESUR
RECTION NOVEMB X
1637
She was the daughter of a former Rector who died in 1641. This is a floor slab.

THE PAINS OF DEATH ARE PAST
LABOUR AND SORROW CEASE
AND LIFES LONG WARFARE CLOSED
THEIR SOULS ARE FOUND IN PEACE
Benjamin Peach of Holyoak d. Aug 27th 1901 Aged 80 years also Hannah, his wife, d. Dec 30th 1903 Aged 82 years. There are many memorials to the Peach family both inside and outside the church. The fine alabaster monument in the church is to Kenelm Digby d. 1590. There are also memorials to the Hamilton-Thompsons, related to Baron Kingsale of the Irish peerage. There is an enclosure in the churchyard to the Bryan family with several Biblical texts.

Stretton St Nicholas

Adieu dear friends till we do meet above,
In Heavens extensive realms of life and love,
We'll bless the Hand Divine that kindly laid
These hearts at rest beneath this secret shade:
But God the Judge will bring to life the dead.,
And all the faithful unto Glory lead;
Thrice blessed bless'd in joyful hope to view,
The cumbrous Body recreated new;
And though the silent tomb shall keep till then secure
May we with rapture rise and never sicken more:
And on the Resurrection day may we rejoice and sing
O grave where is thy victory O Death where is thy sting
James Cross d. Dec 21st 1825 Aged 61 years

A lingering illness thro' this life I've past
With sore consumptive lungs until the last
God sent a messenger; I did obey,
And willingly with him I went away
William Elsom d. February 17th 1854 Aged 30 years

How soon this youth was taken off this stage
By God's decree just in his tender age
Afflicted much, patient in distress,
In hope to gain a future happiness:
O hasty death and fleeting time
To take thee off just in my prime,
It was God's will I'll not complain
We only part to meet again
John Preston d. April 25th 1858 Aged 17 years

Cuthbert Bede, the well-known Victorian author and humorist (1827-1889), is buried in this churchyard. He was actually the Revd Edward Bradley and held the living at Stretton from 1871 to 1883. He died at the age of 62. Also buried here in the impressive family tomb near the west porch is Charles Blake (d. 1791) famous publican at the Ram Jam Inn and inventor of the Ram Jam drink based on a secret recipe.

Teigh Holy Trinity

Young men prepare your self to die
For Life is short and Death is nigh
Prepare in time make no Delay
I in my prime was call'd away
Francis Harris d. June 4th 1780 Aged 22 years

Free from this Dream of life this vale of care
Here rests the Husband kind, the Father dear
In actions faithful and a Friend sincere
Christopher Wright d. Oct 3 1788 Aged 75 years

The best of wives lies buried here,
And loving to her children dear:
Affliction sore with patience bore
Physicians where in vain
Till God did please to me release,
And ease me of my pain
Ann Patchett d. December 17th 1826 Aged 44 years

The perfect love which casts out fear,
To him on earth was given,
Tis but his dust that slumbers here,
His spirit's gone to Heaven
George Flint d. Oct 21ˢᵗ 1856 Aged 78 years

The best of women lies mouldering here
She was loving, to her children dear
And to her Husband a most faithful wife
Until it please'd God for her to depart this life
Anne Hinman d. Nov 24 1871 Aged 46 years

*Anthony Jenkinson, the famous Tudor merchant, diplomat and explorer
who was the first Englishman to penetrate Central Asia(for the
Muscovy Company) died on a visit to his nephew, the Rector of Teigh,
in 1610. He is buried in the churchyard but the location of the grave is
not known. John Banton, village schoolmaster and poet d.1848 is also
buried here. His tombstone is on the right of the pathway to the church.*

Thistleton St Nicholas

OH WE MISS HER BUT HOW SADLY
BLEEDING HEARTS ALONE CAN TELL
EARTH HATH LOST HER HEAVEN HAS FOUND HER
JESUS HATH DONE ALL THINGS WELL
Mary Pettifer d. April 6ᵗʰ 1891

O GOD GIVE ME WORK
TILL MY LIFE SHALL END
AND LIFE
TILL MY WORK IS DONE
Louise Heath d. 20ᵗʰ May 1962 Aged 74 years

Tickencote St Peter

At Floddenfeld did bravely fight and dye
Of Wingfeldes Sonnes y famed Sir Anthonye
But Dethe bee counted mickle gain sith hee
Over ye Scotland gain ye Victorye
Given by John Parry Wingfield in 1938, probably first fixed in
Letheringham church, Suffolk. The battle of Flodden Field was on 9ᵗʰ
September 1513

Deathless principle arise!
Soar thou to thy native skies!
Pearl of price by Jesus bought
To his glorious likeness wrought.
Go to shine before his throne
Deck his mediatorial crown;
Go, his triumph to adorn
Born of God to God return
Rebecca, the wife of Thomas Jelley d. 18ᵗʰ Feb 1842 Aged
31 years

Tinwell All Saints

Farmer and Country Lover
Peter Flint born 28th January 1920 died 5th March 2002

A YOUNG BRITON
David Hallett d. Christmas Day 1971 Aged 17 years

Tixover St Luke

Happy is the man
Who seeks wisdom
And finds understanding
Albert Cecil Steven 7th Feb 1920 – 10th Sept 2000

Uppingham St Peter & St Paul

Here
Lies John Beaver
That honest Man
Which stood up for the
Common of Uppingham
Died November
The 11th 1682

Within this grave a faithful friend's confined
A loving wife and Neighbour kind
A tender Mother, faithful comfort here
Lamented by two children dear
Mourn not your loss
Because to you I was but lent
Kitty Harbutt d. March 22nd 1837 Aged 56 years

INSPIRED
HIS GREAT IDEALS. SHE WAS ALWAYS AN
UNTIRING AND DEVOTED FELLOW WORKER
THROUGH ALL HIS LIFE AT UPPINGHAM
Maria Koch was the wife of Revd Edward Thring. Headmaster of
Uppingham School (1853-87). She died on Sept 20th 1906. This
inscription is on Thring's Celtic cross tombstone in the churchyard.

CYSGWCH MEWN TAWELWCH
Sarah Banner aged 87 years (no date)

Wardley St Botolph

Much lamented Thomas
3rd son of John and Mary WARD
Who was maliciously slain by an Enemy,
Whom he treated with no spite
March 6th 1853 in the 49th year of his age

MORAL IN ALL THE ACTIONS OF HIS LIFE
A FAITHFUL HUSBAND TO A LOVING WIFE
William Mossendue d. April 8th 1847 Aged 78 years

Whissendine St Andrew

Lamented loss. For Thee at Memory's Call
The heart still saddens & the big tears fall
For Thee both Instinct & affection Mourn.
In lisping Infants and in Children Groan:
For Thee the Husband sorrowing
Let sudden Death this moral wide
Religion is the Guardian
Jane Mann who died on the delivery of her nineteenth child
June 30th 1785 Aged 41 years

Weep not for me;
Weep for yourself: for why
I've paid the debt,
But you are still to die
Thomas Gladman d. May 1786 Aged 28 years

A sprightly Youth endowed with manly sense
Til God on high thought fit to call him hence
Duteous he was beloved by friends sincere
But now in sacred dust lies sleeping here
Yet may he rise when bliss supreme is given
And mingle with the Blest the Saints in Heaven
John Walker d. 27th May 1808 Aged 30 years

What faults you've seen in him take care to show
And look at home, enough there's to be done
Death does not always warning give
Therefore be careful how you live
Edward Bree d. July 12th 1827 Aged 56 years

She was-----------------------------
But words are wanting to say what
Think what a Wife should be
She was that
Ann Rimmington Aug 15th 1837 Aged 68 years

Death little warning to us gave,
And quickly sent us to our grave:
Oh! haste to Christ no time delay,
For no one knows their dying day
Charles Toon d. Dec 29th 1844 Aged 56 years & Elizabeth,
his wife, d. Sept 8th 1849 Aged 59 years

I OFTEN LIE AWAKE AT NIGHT
WHEN OTHERS ARE ASLEEP
AND TAKE A WALK DOWN MEMORY LANE
WITH TEARS UPON MY CHEEK
NO ONE KNOWS THE HEARTACHE
I'VE TRIED SO HARD TO HIDE
NO ONE KNOWS HOW MANY TIMES
I'VE BROKEN DOWN AND CRIED
WE SHARE SO MANY HAPPY TIMES
WE SHARE SOME SAD ONES TOO
BUT THE SADDEST IN ALL MY LIFE
WAS THE DAY THAT I LOST YOU *(1987)*

A tiny flower
lent, not given
To bud on earth
and bloom in heaven
Aged 3 months (1996)

WE LIVED TOGETHER AND
WE HAVE GROWN OLD TOGETHER
MANY THANKS FOR A LOVELY MARRIED LIFE
GOD BLESS YOU DEAR *(1999)*

Rest Herein with his Beloved Dog
'Charlie'
A True Gentleman (2003)

Whitwell St Michael & All Angels
NO MORE WE SEE HIM IN OUR MIDST
NO MORE HIS VOICE WE HEAR
FOR DEATH HAS BEEN AND STOLE AWAY
THE ONE WE LOVED SO DEAR
Henry Smith d. Dec 26th 1871 Aged 52 years

AND ART THOU GONE BELOVED ONE
SO EARLY TO THY REST
HOW HARD THE BLOW BUT BE IT SO
FOR TRULY GOD KNOWS BEST
Charles Henry Smith d. June 5th 1873 Aged 28 years

ALARIC
BERNARD JOHN
Who was lost over the
China Sea whilst serving
With the RAF
In Singapore
29.6.1923 – 30.8.1950

Wing St Peter & St Paul

Weep not for me my children dear
God did not please my life to spare
With a tender mother contented be
Therefore prepare to follow me
James Smith Jan 13th 1812

JESUS, MY REDEEMER LIVES,
AND EVER FROM THE SKIES
LOOKS DOWN AND WATCHES ALL MY DUST
TILL HE SHALL BID IT RISE
Sarah Robinson d. November 28th 1859 Aged 52 years

A good life has but few
Days, but a good name
Endureth for ever
*Arthur Frederick Taverner Sec Lieut 1st Battalion King's Shropshire
Light Infantry died of wounds received in the Battle of the Somme
October 11th 1916 Aged 19 years*

Part of the chancel arch, Tickencote

Postcript & Acknowledgements

This selection of epitaphs has been arranged alphabetically and geographically. It could have been arranged in topics or themes such as Human Love, Pain & Sickness, Resignation, Virtue, Humour, Accident & Sudden Death, Faith in God, Duty, War, Hope, Fortitude, Parents & Children, Literary, Integrity, Faithful Wives & Husbands, Ministers, and many more. You may like to look through the collection and see how the epitaphs fit into these headings.

Out of 49 churches visited 10 were closed. Not all these indicated where to find the key. All churchyards were accessible but in the west of the county there are many more slate tombstones than in the east. These preserve the inscriptions very well. Generally, there were many tombstones which could not be read.

Few churches contain epitaphs, the notable exception being Exton. Latin inscriptions have not been included unless a translation had been provided. Occasionally books such as James Wright's *History and Antiquities of the County of Rutland (1684)* and the *Rutland Magazine (1903-08)* contain epitaphs which may now be unreadable in situ.

Though most epitaphs are found on tombstones of the 18th and 19th centuries, there are some very interesting 20th century examples. Where very recent epitaphs have been quoted I have omitted personal details to respect the privacy of people involved.

It would be interesting to know if the stonemasons producing the tombstones (often located in Melton, Leicester or villages like Langham, Rearsby, Hallaton, Billesdon and Uppingham) kept a handbook of epitaphs from which customers could select their choice. Certainly the repetition of some texts suggests this.

Although I have been chastened by the frailty of human mortality in my visits to the graveyards I have also been sustained by the hope expressed in so many epitaphs. A churchyard is a serene and peaceful place mostly well-kept and it is a good place to meditate on the meaning of life and death. Known for centuries as 'God's Acre' it is part of our unique heritage. It has a continuous history of perhaps 1000 years. The inscriptions found there record our social history and they are set in one of our best nature reserves. We should cherish the churchyard whilst we can.

I am grateful to Revd Canon Charles Mayhew for writing the Foreword. Also to Mr PK Rollings and Egleton Church for permission to use his excellent sketches of the stonework on the front cover. The companionship, advice and photography of my wife Beryl have been of inestimable value to me which I appreciate very much.

'So one is set for a good morning among the churches: not more than three in a morning is sufficient for enjoyment, and perhaps another one or two after tea: and the afternoon spent in the field in the Midland sun, quiet, unwinding'
W G Hoskins: Rutland A Shell Guide (1963)

Love not thyself the less, although the least thou art.
What thou in greatness wants, wise Nature doth impart
In goodness of thy Soyl; and more delicious Mould,
Surveying all this Ile, the Sun did ne're behold.
Bring forth that British Vale, and be it ne're so rare,
But **Catmus** with that Vale for richness may compare,
What Forest Nymph is found, how brave so ere she be,
But **Lyfeild** shews her self as brave a Nymph as she?
What River ever rose from Bank. or swelling Hill,
Then **Rutlands** wandring **Wash**, a delicater Rill?
Small Shire that canst produce to thy proportion good,
One Vale of Special Name, one Forest, and one Flood.
O **Catmus**, thou fair Vale, come on in Grass and Corn,
That **Beaver** ne're be said thy sisterhood to scorn,
And let thy **Ocham** boast to have no little Grace,
That her the pleased Fates did in thy Bosom place:
And **Lifeild**, as thou art a Forest, live so free,
That every Forest-Nymph may praise the sports in thee:
And down to **Wellends** course, O **Wash**, run ever cleer,
To honour, and to be much honour'd by this Shire

Michael Drayton in *Polyolbion (1613)*